WORLD OF INSECTS

# Moths

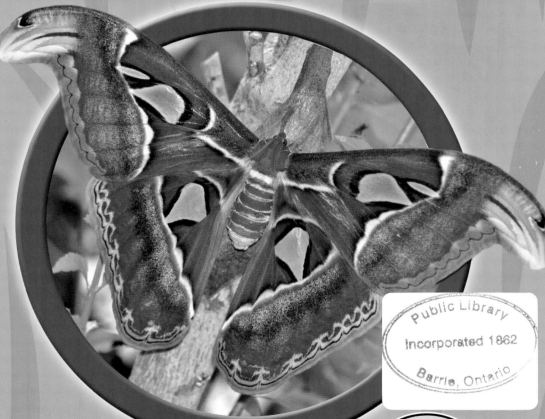

by Martha E. H. Rustad

BELLWETHER MEDIA • MINNEAPOLIS, MN

Note to Librarians, Teachers, and Parents:

**Blastoff! Readers** are carefully developed by literacy experts and combine standards-based content with developmentally-appropriate text.

**Level 1** provides the most support through repetition of high-frequency words, light text, predictable sentence patterns, and strong visual support.

**Level 2** offers early readers a bit more challenge through varied simple sentences, increased text load, and less repetition of high frequency words.

**Level 3** advances early-fluent readers toward fluency through increased text and concept load, less reliance on visuals, longer sentences, and more literary language.

**Level 4** builds reading stamina by providing more text per page, increased use of punctuation, greater variation in sentence patterns, and increasingly challenging vocabulary.

**Level 5** encourages children to move from "learning to read" to "reading to learn" by providing even more text, varied writing styles, and less familiar topics.

Whichever book is right for your reader, Blastoff! Readers are the perfect books to build confidence and encourage a love of reading that will last a lifetime!

This edition first published in 2008 by Bellwether Media.

No part of this publication may be reproduced in whole or in part without written permission of the publisher. For information regarding permission, write to Bellwether Media Inc., Attention: Permissions Department, Post Office Box 1C, Minnetonka, MN 55345-9998.

Library of Congress Cataloging-in-Publication Data
Rustad, Martha E. H. (Martha Elizabeth Hillman), 1975–
  Moths / by Martha E.H. Rustad.
    p. cm. – (Blastoff! readers. World of insects)
Summary: "Simple text accompanied by full-color photographs give an upclose look at moths. Intended for kindergarten through third grade students"—Provided by publisher.
  Includes bibliographical references and index.
  ISBN-13: 978-1-60014-107-2 (hardcover : alk. paper)
  ISBN-10: 1-60014-107-2 (hardcover : alk. paper)
  1. Moths–Juvenile literature. I. Title.

QL544.2.R88 2008
595.78–dc22                                    2007009765

# Contents

Moths are **insects**. Most moths fly at night and rest during the day.

Moths live in every part of the world except **Antarctica**.

Moths hatch from eggs.
They start life as **caterpillars**.

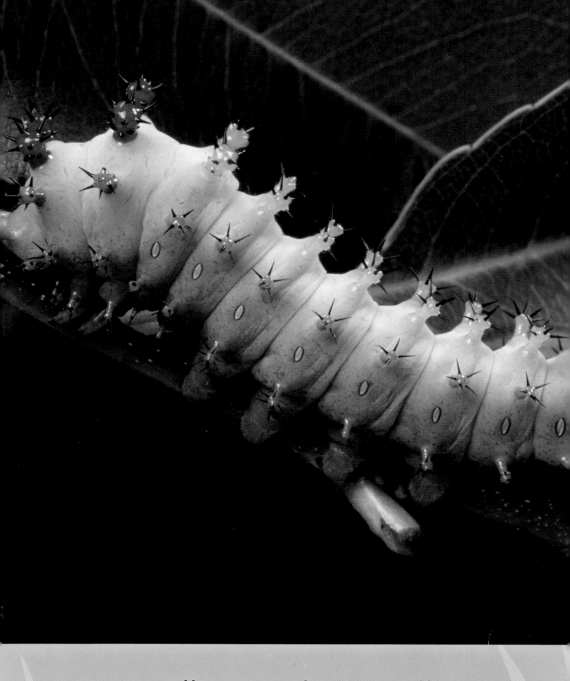

Caterpillars eat leaves all day long. They grow quickly.

Caterpillars make **silk** thread inside their bodies.

A full-grown caterpillar
wraps silk around its body.
It makes a **cocoon**.

The caterpillar stays inside
the cocoon for many days.
It changes into a moth.

10

Soon the moth wiggles out
of the cocoon.

A moth has four wings.
Colored **scales** cover
the wings.

Many moths are brown or gray. This helps them **blend** in with their surroundings.

Some moths have
brighter colors.

Some have spots on their wings.
The spots look like big eyes.
They scare away **predators**.

Most moths drink **nectar**
from flowers.

Most moths have a mouth shaped like a straw. They suck nectar through it.

antennas

Moths have two hairy **antennas**.

Moths use their antennas to smell. This helps them find nectar.

A male moth uses its antennas to find a female by its smell.

The female lays eggs.
Soon new moth caterpillars
will hatch.

# Glossary

**Antarctica**—the continent covering the South Pole

**antennas**—a pair of thin feelers on an insect's head

**blend**—to mix with something else; moths mix with their surroundings to hide.

**caterpillar**—a young moth that looks like a worm

**cocoon**—a silk covering that protects a caterpillar as it changes into a moth

**insect**—a kind of animal with six legs; most insects also have a hard body, two antennas, and two or four wings.

**nectar**—sweet juice made by flowers

**predator**—an animal that hunts and kills other animals

**scales**—tiny colored plates on the wings of a moth

**silk**—a soft material made inside the bodies of some caterpillars

# To Learn More

## AT THE LIBRARY

Helget, Nicole. *Moths*. Mankato, Minn.: Creative Education, 2007.

Loewen, Nancy. *Night Fliers: Moths in your Backyard*. Minneapolis, Minn.: Picture Window Books, 2004.

Macken, JoAnn Early. *The Life Cycle of a Moth*. Milwaukee, Wis.: Weekly Reader, 2006.

## ON THE WEB

Learning more about moths is as easy as 1, 2, 3.

1. Go to www.factsurfer.com

2. Enter "moths" into search box.

3. Click the "Surf" button and you will see a list of related web sites.

With factsurfer.com, finding more information is just a click away.

# Index

The photographs in this book are reproduced through the courtesy of: Maggie, front cover; Dianne McFadden, p. 4; Altrendo Nature/Getty Images, pp. 5, 11, 12, 14, 15, 16, 19, 20; Graphic Science/Alamy, p. 6; George Grall/Getty Images, p. 7; Cathy Keifer, p. 8; blickwinkel/Alamy, pp. 9, 10, 21; Alexander M. Omelko, p. 13, Woodfall Wild Images/Alamy, p. 17; Bruce McQueen, p. 18.